SIXTY MILLION YEARS OF HORSES

by Lois and Louis Darling

WILLIAM MORROW AND COMPANY NEW YORK 1960

Published simultaneously in the Dominion of
Canada by George J. McLeod Limited, Toronto.

Printed in the United States of America.

Library of Congress Catalog Card Number 60-8998

* *

Probably no other animal has inspired so much writing, painting, sculpture, and photography as the horse. Great scientists have spent years of work and study on the horse. Horses were pictured as part of the human story almost as soon as man could make a picture.

Men are rather weak, awkward, and slow of foot when compared to other animals. In horses man found strength and speed, which he could use. Here was the beauty of rippling muscles and grace of body, which he could admire. In the long history of the companionship between man and horse, its beauty has been as important as its usefulness.

Today machines have almost entirely taken the place of the horse. Tractors have replaced the plow horse, automobiles the coach and saddle horse, and trucks the wagon horses. Tanks, jeeps, and other machines have made cavalry obsolete in modern warfare. Nowadays the horse is valued almost entirely for its beauty and for the companionship and sport it provides.

In the United States there are now more than two and one half million horses. All over the country, young and old ride over two hundred thousand horses just for the fun of it. There are one hundred and fifty thousand Thoroughbred race horses and one hundred thousand trotting race horses. Horse races draw millions in attendance. There are hundreds of horse shows, small and large, every year.

Rodeos are popular, because of the fine working cow horses used in them. In the West the horse is often the best means of handling cattle. In rough country saddle and pack horses can carry men and their baggage where no machine can go. If you have ever been to an old-time country fair, you know that many farmers still have pride in the strength and beauty of their great draft horses and the smartness and speed of their trotters.

Today's autos and fast trains are making it possible for more people to work in the cities and live in the suburbs or country, where they have room to keep animals. So Shetland ponies are becoming popular. There are more of these little horses today than ever before, at least one hundred and thirty thousand of them. Burros are also having a boom. Both ponies and burros can even be bought from mail order houses! It is strange that automobiles and trains, which put so many horses out of work, should be responsible for the increasing popularity of the world's smallest horses.

So far we have been speaking of horses in a general way. There are several different kinds, or species, of horses in addition to the domestic animal we usually refer to as the horse. There are onagers, wild asses, and three species of zebras, all of which are, strictly speaking, horses. All these, as well as domestic horses, belong to the group, or genus, *Equus.* To distinguish the species to which true horses belong from all these other species, science has added the word *caballus* to the name *Equus,* making *Equus caballus* the scientific name of the species to which domestic horses belong.

ONAGER–EQUUS HEMIONUS

WILD ASS – EQUUS ASINUS

GRÉVY'S ZEBRA – EQUUS GRÉVYI

There are no truly wild horses in North or South America. The wild horses of our western plains are the descendants of domestic horses which escaped and went wild many years ago. But in prehistoric and early historic times truly wild horses were plentiful all through Europe and central Asia. They were called tarpans and in eastern Russia they may have still roamed free in the early nineteen hundreds. They are now all extinct.

The only genuinely wild *Equus caballus* that may still exist is the central Asiatic horse named after its discoverer with the unpronounceable Russian name, Przewalski. Even this last really wild horse may now be extinct and gone forever from the wild countries of Mongolia and Turkestan where it used to roam.

TARPANS

During all the long history of man's use of the horse, he has recognized natural differences among horses which made them useful for doing different kinds of work or giving people pleasure. These characteristics have been preserved by carefully breeding together only the horses which had them.

For instance, a horse might be born which was a little bigger and stronger than most other horses. This animal would be bred only to another horse which was also bigger and stronger. Their colts would also be big and strong. When this sort of selective breeding was continued generation after generation, great horses, such as the Shires and Percherons, were finally developed. Whatever man wanted in his horses—fleetness, strength, or smallness—he could produce by long years of selective breeding. The different breeds of horses we have today all originated in this way.

The most important breeds of light horses in America are the Arabian, the Thoroughbred, the American Quarter Horse, the Morgan, the Standard-Bred trotter, the Hackney, the American Saddle Horse, the Tennessee Walking Horse, and the Cleveland Bay. The heavy draft horses are the Percheron, the Belgian, the Clydesdale, the Shire, and the Suffolk. The famous palomino is not as yet a regular pure breed. Palomino colts do not always have the beautiful golden color of their parents. However, breeders are trying to establish palominos as purebred horses by selective breeding, and they may be successful in doing so someday.

ARABIAN

THOROUGHBRED

MORGAN

STANDARD-BRED

HACKNEY

AMERICAN SADDLE HORSE

TENNESSEE WALKING HORSE

PERCHERON

SHETLAND SHIRE
(THE SMALLEST AND THE LARGEST)

MULE
CROSS BETWEEN MALE ASS AND MARE

PALOMINO

Today breeds are carefully kept up to standards. When a colt is born it is usually registered, so there is a record of its ancestry, or pedigree. All such registered horses are called purebred. You often hear people say thoroughbred when they mean purebred. They also sometimes say a dog is thoroughbred. A dog cannot be a thoroughbred. Thoroughbred is the name for a breed of racehorses only. Thoroughbred and purebred do not mean the same thing.

Many fine horses come from the breeding of a purebred horse with another of unknown ancestry. These are called grade horses. Our departments of agriculture, both state and federal, keep many fine purebred stallions of various breeds in different localities, so that farmers and ranchers may use them to breed with their mares to obtain colts with better qualities. Of course, many fine and useful horses have unknown ancestry on both sides.

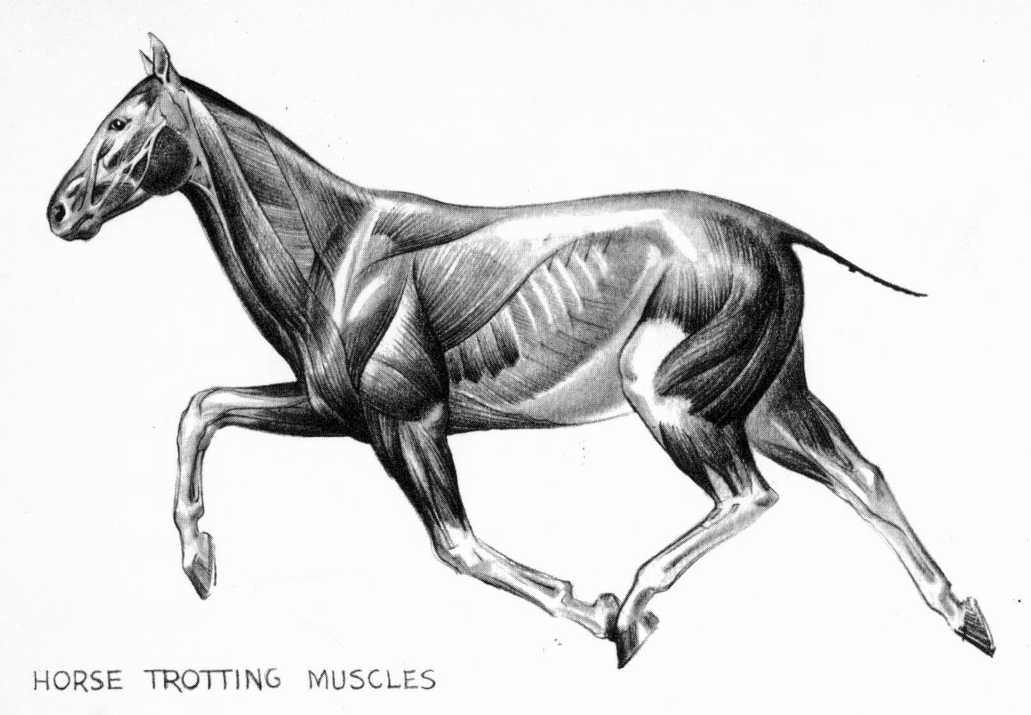
HORSE TROTTING MUSCLES

All living things are fitted to suit the way in which they live. Natural wild horses are suited for their life on the open plains and a diet of tough grass. They have the ability to escape from enemies by means of great speed over hard ground. The horse's tremendous running muscles are bunched at the upper parts of its legs. The lower parts are long, light levers that can reach out in a long stride with as little effort and movement of muscles as possible. This long stride is lengthened still more, since the horse stands on the very tips of its single toes. These toes are covered by strong, sharp hoofs, which the horse can dig in to get a sure grip on hard ground. You lengthen your stride in somewhat the same way when you stand up on your toes to run.

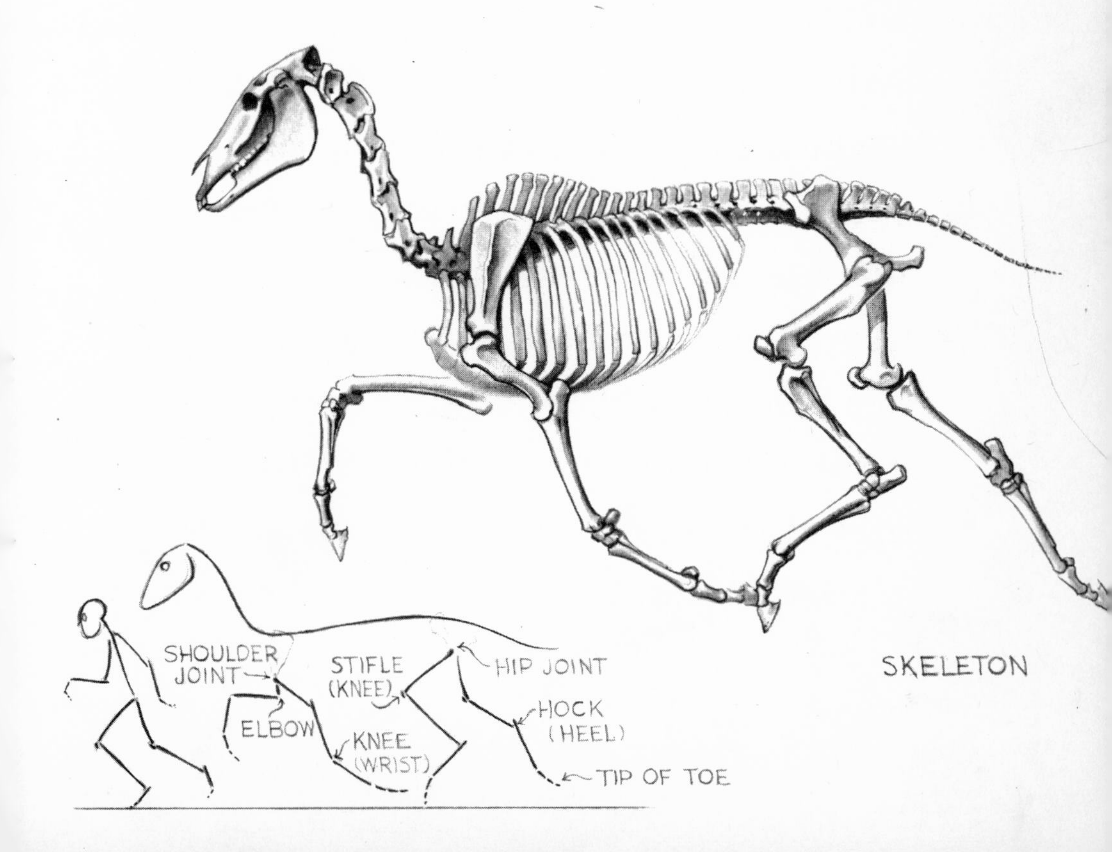

The horse's long neck makes it possible for it to reach its grassy food while standing straight on all four legs, ready to run. Its large eyes are set high on its head, so that when it thrusts its long muzzle deep in the grass it still can see the slightest movement around it. The horse's eyes are also placed more on the side of its head, rather than in the front as yours are. So it can see in front and behind quite well, without having to move its head. A horse's eyesight is its most important sense, but its smell and hearing are also very keen. So the horse is always on the alert and ready to use its blazing speed to keep itself from harm.

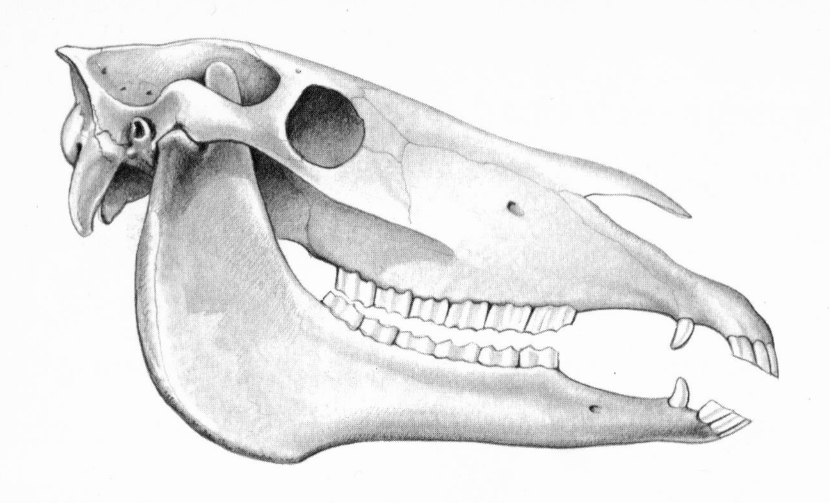

The teeth of the horse are most important bits of living machinery completely adapted to eating grass. Grass is a food that is very wearing on the teeth. It contains tiny particles of silica, which is an abrasive material. If a human being had to live on grass, his teeth would wear down to the gums in a couple of years. A grown horse has twelve front teeth, or incisors, six below and six above. With the help of its flexible, sensitive lips, the horse cuts grass with these curved nippers. Male horses have a small, pointed canine tooth behind the incisors. Next there is a toothless space in the mouths of both male and female. This space is very convenient for man, for in it he places the bit used in domestic horses. Adult horses, after four or five years, have a complete set of cheek, or grinding, teeth following this space. There are six of these teeth in each side of the upper and lower jaw —twenty-four in all. These all look almost exactly alike, except that the first three are a little bit more triangular than the last three. The reason for this slight difference is that the first three are premolars, while the last three are true molars. This fact is very important in the study of the ancestors of horses and how their teeth changed through the ages to enable them to live on a grass diet.

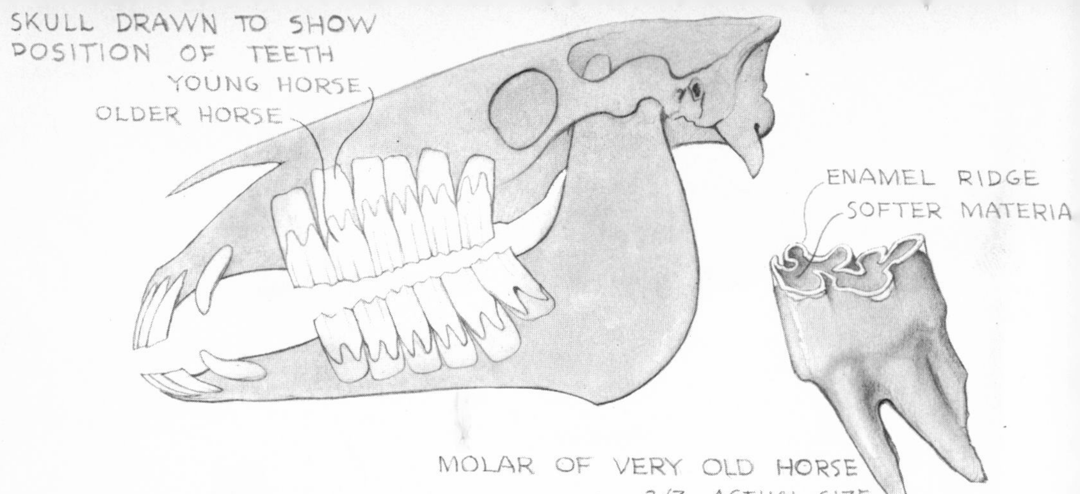

A horse's cheek teeth are very long. When the horse is young, most of the length is embedded in the bones of the jaw. But as the harsh grass wears the teeth down, they move outward so that their grinding surfaces are always at the same level. These grinding surfaces have a complicated pattern made up of low ridges of hard enamel. These stand up above a material which is softer than the enamel. As the tooth wears, the hard enamel ridges do not wear down as fast as the softer material, so that the grinding surface does not become smooth with age. The next time you

have a chance to watch a horse eat, notice the circular grinding motion of its jaws as it pulverizes its food between the rough surfaces of its cheek teeth.

The brain of a horse is large as animal brains go. However, the smartest horse is not nearly as intelligent as any human being. The horse uses its brain mainly to direct the wonderful balance and quick motions of its strong body. Horses are born knowing how to do many things by inherited instinct. They do other things by learned habit, but are not able to reason very much.

A great deal of man's interest in horses is scientific. The fossil record of the horse is marvelously complete. It plainly shows the slow changes that have taken place in the horse through millions and millions of years—the changes we call evolution. Even if horses were important for no other reason, they would be famous animals because of this wonderful record of changing life.

The most important part of horse evolution took place in North America. In starting to talk about it, we must use the Greek word *hippos,* which means horse. Another Greek

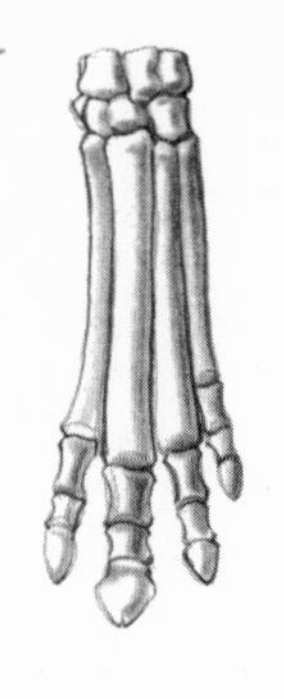

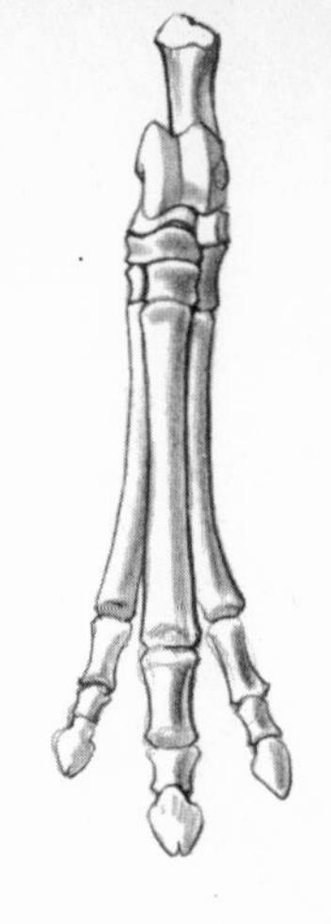

word *eo,* means dawn. Put the two together, as scientists often do when naming animals and plants, and we have eohippus, the dawn, or beginning, horse. The fossil record of horses starts with eohippus, which lived seventy-five million years ago, long after the dinosaurs had disappeared from the world. There were many eohippus species, and hundreds of their fossil skeletons have been found. They were little animals about as big as foxes. Their legs were long and slender, and they had four toes on their front feet and three toes on their back feet. Each toe was tipped with a tiny hoof.

Eohippus' molars and premolars had begun to develop the special grinding surface of those of plant-eating animals, but these cheek teeth were still quite short. They would not have lasted long on a grass diet. The dawn horses

were pretty little animals, which lived in woodsy places and ate the tender leaves of shrubs and herbs. Animals which eat this sort of plant food are called browsers, while animals which eat grass are called grazers.

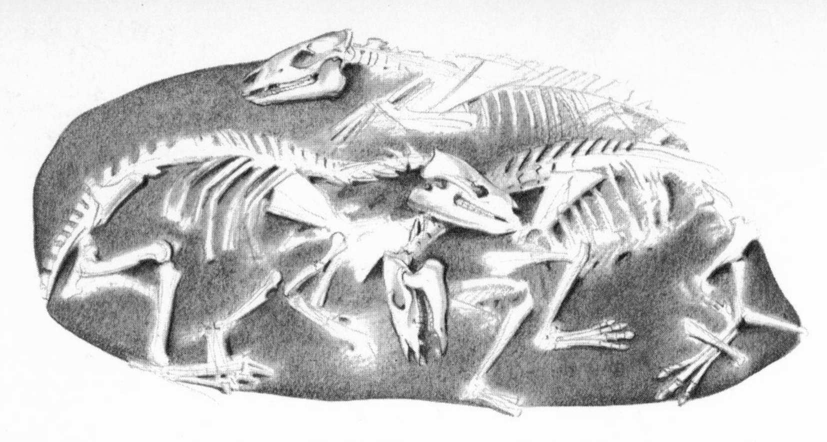

Thousands of different fossils have been found which show the many different steps in evolution that led from eohippus to *Equus.* They show us that horses evolved in three important lines. The horses in the first line remained browsers as long as they lasted, and had three hoofed toes on each foot. The horses in the second line became adapted to a grazing way of life, and also had three hoofed toes on each foot. The third kind were grazers too, but lost all but one toe on each foot. This last is the line of horses whose living representative is *Equus.* The two other lines of horses have long been extinct.

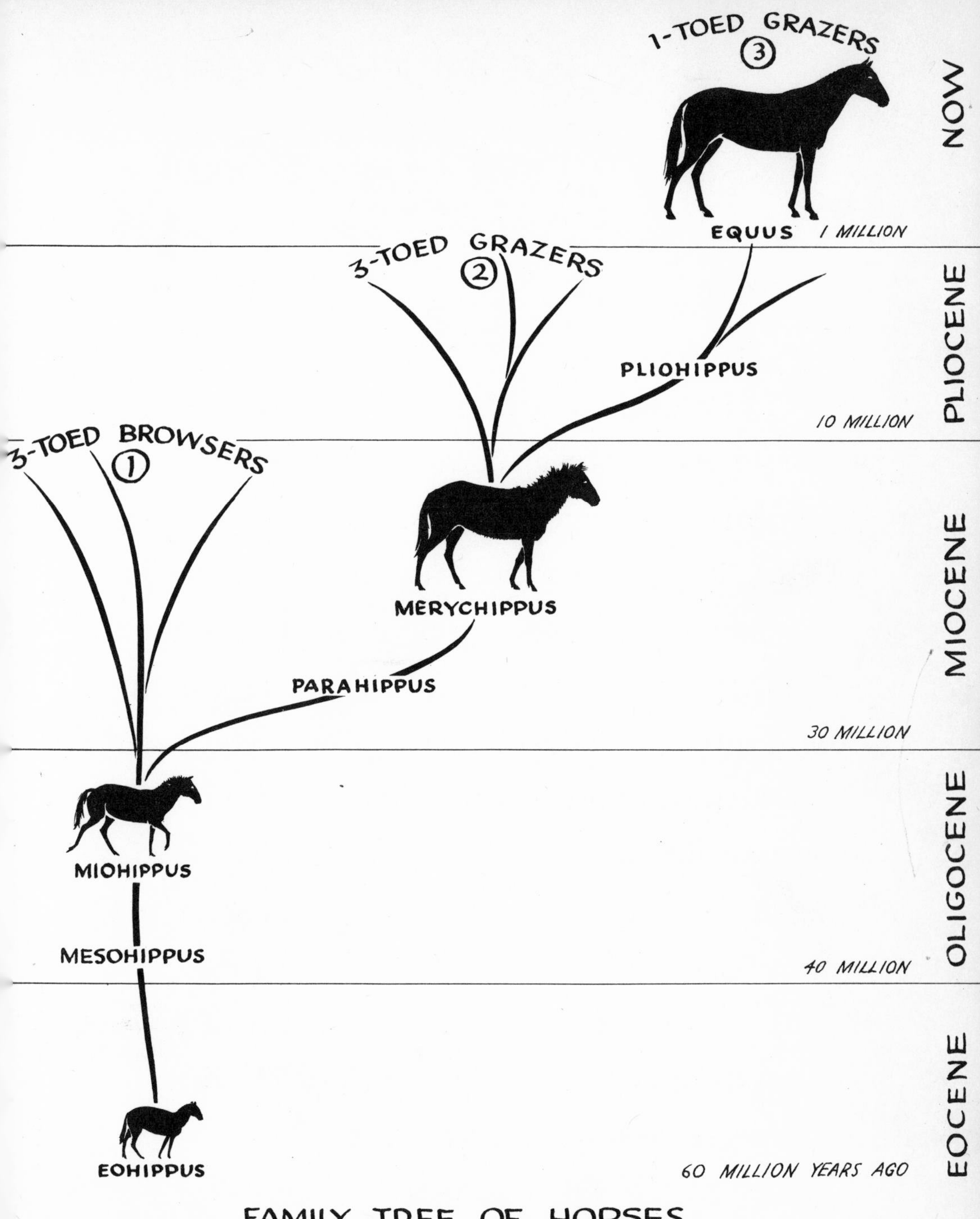

FAMILY TREE OF HORSES

The horse that evolved from eohippus in the first line of evolution was *Mesohippus,* which means middle horse. It had only three toes on its front feet instead of the four that eohippus had. The outside toe had disappeared, but left its traces as a little nubbin of bone, which can be seen in its fossils. *Mesohippus* lived about forty million years ago in the Oligocene epoch. Its head was more horselike than that of eohippus, and the lower parts of its legs were longer. *Mesohippus'* teeth were short and suitable for browsing. But the three premolars had become much like the molars, and together they made up a set of grinding

MESOHIPPUS

MIOHIPPUS 28"

cheek teeth that became typical of all horses.

Miohippus, which came along later in the Oligocene epoch, was a descendant of *Mesohippus.* It was a bit larger than *Mesohippus* and was just a bit more like the modern horse. This browsing line kept on evolving into other species. They probably lived in forests, wet lands, or along the banks of rivers. On the soft soil of such places the wide, three-toed feet were an advantage. These browsing horses flourished all over North America, Europe, and Asia for millions of years. They all became extinct about five or ten million years ago, and they have left no direct descendants.

In the meantime, the first grazing horses, in the second line of evolution, branched off from the browsers. These were descendants of *Miohippus.* Two important horses in this group were *Parahippus* and *Merychippus.* They were the first horses in which the long grass-grinding cheek teeth appeared. Because of this new kind of teeth, horses were able to live in the spreading grasslands of that time. Here was a new way and place in which horses could live, where there was food and space. So grazing horses multiplied enormously. Some *Merychippus* species reached a height of forty inches, as tall as a medium-sized Shetland pony. Their skulls became much like those of modern horses with the familiar deep jaws necessary for holding the long teeth. Both *Parahippus* and *Merychippus* had three toes on each foot. As time went on, two of these toes became smaller and smaller, and most of the animal's weight was supported by the large central hoof. The small side hoofs acted only as shock absorbers when the horse came down extra hard on its feet when running or jumping. If you could have seen *Merychippus,* with its feet covered by long grass, you would have thought you were looking at a small modern horse. But no human being ever saw *Merychippus* alive. Even the earliest of cave men had not yet appeared on earth.

MERYCHIPPUS 40"

These three-toed grazers went on evolving and branched off into many slightly different species. They spread all over the world except for Australia, which they could not reach, because it was an island continent. The last of the three-toed grazers lived in Africa and became extinct only about half a million years ago.

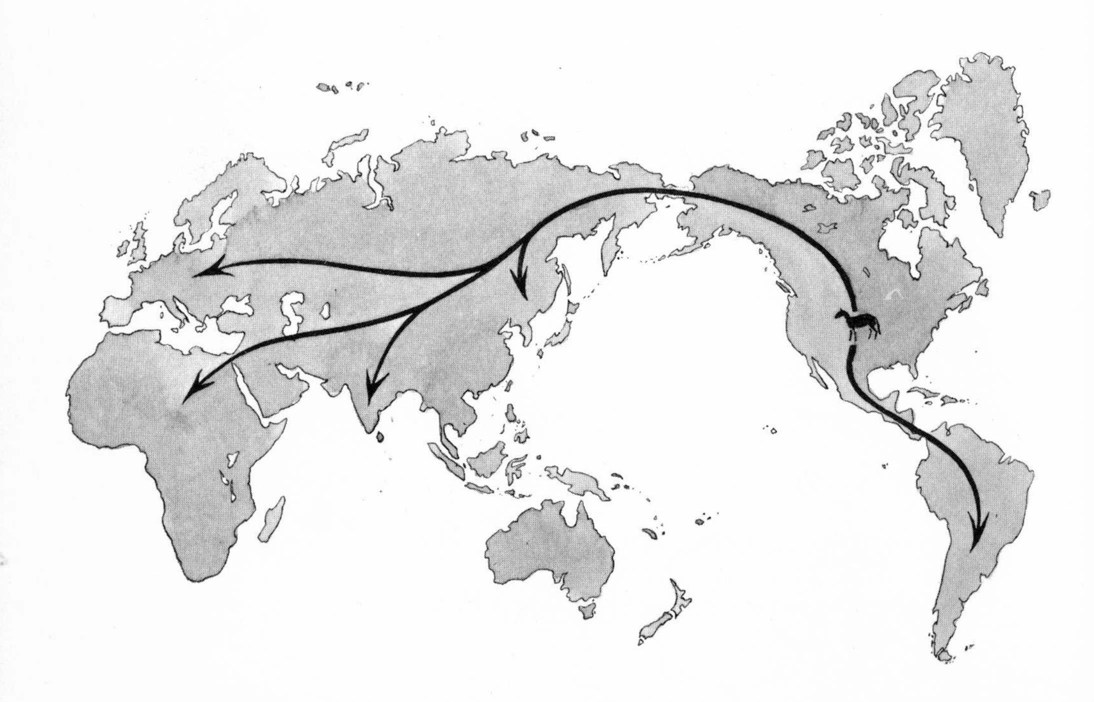

THE SPREAD OF EARLY HORSES

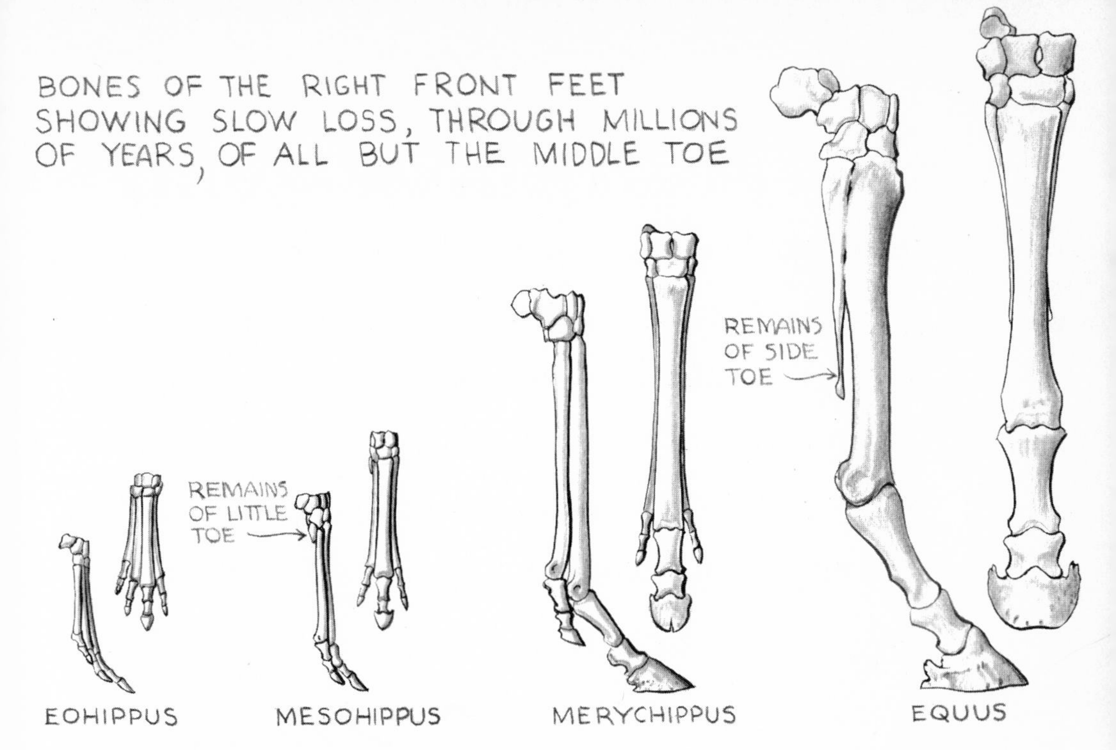

Merychippus was also the ancestor of the horses in the third line of evolution, the one-toed grazers, which led to modern horses. An early descendant of *Merychippus* was *Pliohippus.* Its two side toes became so small that they were entirely useless, and its teeth became better adapted for grazing. Later species of *Pliohippus* were almost exactly like modern horses, except for a few small details.

Soon *Equus* evolved in North America and migrated to South America. It also traveled to the Old World over a land route between Alaska and Russia, which existed at that time. The land route then slowly sank beneath the sea and the Americas became cut off from the Old World as they are today. *Equus* then became completely extinct in the Americas. Why this happened is as great a mystery to science as is the great world-wide extinction of the dinosaurs, which took place about seventy-five million years earlier. Other animals also became extinct in the Western Hemisphere during these same years. Changes which we do not yet understand made it impossible for such animals as sabertooths, great ground sloths, mastodons, and camels to survive. All of them became extinct along with the horses.

Imagine camels or great lumbering mastodons
living, perhaps, where you live now.

But *Equus* continued to thrive in Europe, Asia, and Africa. Somewhere along the years he was met by man. The history of man's connection with horses began a long, long time ago. In the beautiful cave paintings of Europe, pictures of horses are common. These paintings were made by Cro-Magnon men at least twenty thousand years ago. The men of

this time were hunters. In France there is a great Cro-Magnon trash heap. In it are the bones of over a hundred thousand horses. There are many other such sites of remains left by ancient men that show that they probably thought of horses only in terms of stew and steak.

Horses must have first been tamed by later roaming tribes of hunters in Europe and Asia. Dogs had long been domesticated by these people to help them with their hunting and to guard their camp sites. So the idea of taming a wild horse would have occurred naturally to these wild nomadic people. Probably a boy wanted a pet or a girl wanted to mother some young animal, and found a little colt, which had been orphaned when its mother was killed for food in a horse hunt. The boy's or girl's parents may have scolded or laughed at first. But the colt ate only grass and nothing that was useful to the tribe for food. As it grew into a strong animal, it was quickly discovered how useful it could be to a wandering people. A tame horse was such a fine idea that it must have spread like wildfire through

the lonely forests and plains of long-ago Europe and Asia. Horses must have soon been domesticated in many different places. Those with different qualities were probably exchanged between tribes. The first horse breeding and horse trading went on before recorded history.

A MOSAIC FROM THE CITY OF UR, 4500 YEARS OLD

The first historical record of horses as domestic animals appears in the art of ancient Mesopotamian civilizations, which flourished more than two thousand years before the birth of Christ. In this area of the Near East men had first learned to raise crops and keep other domestic animals, like the goat, pig, ox, and sheep. The extra food this gave them released them from the endless toil of hunting and

THESE ANIMALS WERE PROBABLY ONAGERS

made it possible to build cities, and have extra time for such things as art. They learned to write, to read, and to keep records of events. They established trade with other peoples. Here was the beginning of recorded history and the birthplace of European civilization. Horses probably came to Mesopotamia in trade from southeastern Europe, as there were few wild horses in the Near East area.

ANCIENT CHARIOT AND ONAGERS

When we think of horses today we think of them in connection with work or sport. But the biggest use of horses for many centuries after their domestication was in war. Horses have been mixed up in man's bloody squabbles since the dawn of recorded history. In the earliest Mesopotamian pictures horses almost always appear pulling a war chariot. Oxen and asses were the work animals.

The use of heavy, massed war chariots made a series of great Near Eastern nations almost unconquerable until Alexander the Great, from Macedonia, changed the tactics of war about 330 B.C. His cavalry consisted of bowmen mounted on light, fast horses. It could easily out-maneuver the clumsy chariots. Alexander won battle after battle and conquered the civilized world of the time.

ALEXANDER AND HIS FAMOUS HORSE, BUCEPHALUS

In the days of chivalry, during the European Middle Ages, the horse was as much a part of the scene as was the knight. The word *chivalry* comes from the French word for horse, *cheval.*

As time went on, the knights dressed themselves and their war horses in more and heavier armor. To carry all this extra weight they had to breed their horses to be bigger and stronger. The result was the Great Horse of the European Middle Ages. These great chargers were the mounts in war as well as in tournaments when rival knights rode full tilt at each other with lances. The object was to knock the opposing knight off his horse and win the hand of some fair lady. The clanking crash when one of these warriors "hit the dust" must have been some-

thing to remember! These war horses of the Middle Ages were highly valued, perhaps more than the knights. Tournament rules stated that a knight must never wound the horse of his opponent with lance, sword, or mace, but must use these weapons only on the person of the other knight.

During the crusades hundreds of thousands of knights rode their Great Horses to the Holy Land. Here they met Near Eastern warriors mounted on their light, fast horses and whirling sharp scimitars over their heads. It never has been clear which side came out the winner in this clash of armored knight on his powerful horse against eastern swordsman on his light, fast mount. Both sides won and lost innumerable battles. But the crusades did introduce eastern ways and eastern horses to Europe in the Middle Ages.

With the end of the Middle Ages and chivalry, the armored knights disappeared and their horses went to work. But the Great Horses were no less noble because of this change. They became the fine, powerful draft horses that did so much useful work until just a few short years ago. The ancestors of the Percheron, the Belgian, the Shire, the Clydesdale, and the other beautiful draft breeds of today were the chargers of the knights of old.

The oldest breed of light riding horses is the famous Arabian. This breed was well established in the days of Mohammed, about 620 A.D., and has changed little since then. Today many horse fanciers think the Arabian is the finest of all. This breed doubtless descended from older Near Eastern horses. Egyptian, Assyrian, and Greek art show horses with many Arabian features.

The desert Bedouins, who developed them, bred Arabian horses to suit their hard, wandering, warlike lives. Like all great horsemen through the ages, they valued their mounts above everything else. An Arabian saying is, "Every grain of barley given to a horse is entered by God in the Register of Good Works."

A breed similar to the Arabian is the Barb, which originated in North Africa west of Egypt in the section that used to be called Barbary. Both Barbs and Arabians are tremendously important, because they have been crossed with the horses of other lands for centuries, and have improved their quality. There are almost no light horses anywhere that do not have some Arabian or Barb ancestors.

The great Mohammedan conquest was possible only because of these wonderful horses. It threatened to overrun Europe when the Mohammedans conquered most of Spain. The conquest was not halted until 732 A.D. when European knights defeated the Mohammedans in France. During this time the invaders' horses were interbred with Spanish horses, and a splendid light horse, the jennet, was the result.

After Columbus discovered America, Spanish conquistadores explored the New World.

They, as well as later Spanish settlers, had jennets with them. Many of these horses escaped and multiplied on our western plains and on the pampas of South America. In North America these domestic horses that had become wild were called mustangs, from the Spanish word *mesteño,* which means wild. Indians captured many mustangs. Spanish horses were traded to, or stolen by, the Indians. They took naturally to the horse and became great riders. Before 1700 nearly all the tribes of the western half of North America had horses.

The Indian pony was one of the finest kinds of mustangs. The mustangs did not resemble their ancestors, the jennets or the proud Arabians, very much. They were smallish, ragged, wiry animals. But they were incredibly tough, intelligent, and well able to stand the hard conditions of the early wild West.

The mustang has since been interbred with many other breeds of horses and is practically extinct today. But its heritage lives on in many western cow ponies. These horses were the first to live in the Western Hemisphere since *Equus* had mysteriously become extinct so long ago.

The Spanish jennet also spread to other countries in Europe and was bred with local horses. So it introduced the qualities of the Arabian and Barb horses in Europe as well as in America. There is a record, too, of a pure Arabian horse's being imported to England as early as 1100. Starting in about 1600, Arabian horses were regularly imported to England for the purpose of improving English breeds. It was in England that the beautiful Thoroughbred breed originated. The ancestry of every Thoroughbred that lives today can be traced back over two hundred years through a maze of ancestors to three Near Eastern stallions—the Byerly Turk, 1689, the Darley Arabian, 1700, and the Goldolphin Barb, 1730. These three stallions were bred to English mares, which already contained much

Arabian heredity, and their offspring became the Thoroughbred breed. The Thoroughbred was selectively bred for speed and is the fastest runner of all horses. It is also through the Thoroughbreds, as they were crossed with many other breeds and types of horses, that the Arabian heredity has been spread so far and wide. The American Saddle Horse, the Morgan, the Quarter Horse, the Standard-Bred trotter, and the Tennessee Walking Horse are all famous American breeds which have Thoroughbred horses in their ancestry.

So the qualities of the splendid desert horses, the Arabians and Barbs, have been spread to many lands through the centuries. In early American colonial times, for example, horses from England were crossed with local horses of Spanish jennet ancestry. These horses were bred to thrive in the hard conditions of pioneer times. The pioneers also raced them, but they did not have large, costly race tracks. One type of horse was developed to race over their short, rough tracks which were only

about a quarter of a mile in length. These horses became known for their terrific speed over short distances. The famous American breed, the Quarter Horse, originated from these early pioneer racers. Today Quarter Horses—tough, agile, and tremendously fast for short distances—make perhaps the best cow ponies and polo ponies of any breed.

ICELAND PONY

Quite different from all these noble horses of the past and present are the modern descendants of the little Celtic pony. It was small, about forty-five inches at the shoulders. It was a sturdy horse, probably descended without much change from the original small, wild European horse. Its remains have been found in many prehistoric sites. The Iceland pony is probably the least changed of the descendants of the Celtic pony. But the Celtic pony was also the ancestor of the Welsh pony and the little lovable Shetland pony.

Slowly, through millions and millions of years of evolution, the horse became adapted into a wonderful, fleet, tough creature of the open plains. Through the centuries man has molded this animal to suit his special needs. The mighty Percheron, the tough and beautiful Arabian, the quick, sturdy Quarter Horse, the speedy Thoroughbred, the little Shetland, and many other different breeds and types have all played an important part in man's adventures, work, and pleasures. Now the fam-

iliar horse is gone from the city streets and the farmer's fields. No longer do beautiful, dashing fire horses answer the alarm. No longer do farm horses pull loads of sweet-smelling hay along country lanes. Gone are the horse-drawn sleighs in winter, the doctor's horse and buggy, the milkman's horse that knew the route and stops better than its master did, and all the horses that were such a familiar part of the lives of your parents and grandparents. But the horse is still with us in spite of the fact that it is no longer very useful. As long as human beings care about beautiful animals for their own sakes, the horse will be part of the human story.